APR 07 2014

j796.522 H994c
Conquering Everest /
Hyde, Natalie,

WITHDRAWN

D0460914

# CONQUERING EVEREST

## Natalie Hyde

CRABTREE
Publishing Company
www.crabtreebooks.com

# Crabtree Publishing Company
## www.crabtreebooks.com

**Author:** Natalie Hyde
**Publishing plan research
    and development:** Reagan Miller
**Editors:** Sonya Newland, Kathy Middleton
**Proofreader:** Crystal Sikkens
**Photo Researcher:** Sonya Newland
**Original design:** Tim Mayer
    (Mayer Media)
**Book design:** Kim Williams
    (320 Media)
**Cover design:** Ken Wright
**Production coordinator and
    prepress tecnician:** Ken Wright
**Print coordinator:** Margaret Amy Salter

Produced for Crabtree Publishing
Company by White-Thomson Publishing

**Photographs:**
Alamy: Pictorial Press Ltd: pp. 18–19; Corbis:
pp. 3, 14–15; HO/Reuters: pp. 1, 37; Hulton-
Deutsch Collection: p. 20; Christian Kober/
JAI: pp. 38–39; Getty Images: pp. 26–27, 32,
34–35; Time & Life Pictures: p. 16; Popperfoto:
p. 33; Shutterstock: zagart116: back cover;
Arsgera: pp. 4–5; My Good Images: pp. 6–7;
Daniel Prudek: pp. 8, 28–29; Vadim Petrakov:
pp. 9, 12, 24–25; Bruce Yeung: p. 10; Zzvet:
pp. 11, 43, 44–45; SIHASAKPRACHUM: pp.
22–23, 40–41; Galyna Andrushko: p. 25; Jose
Fuente : p. 42; SuperStock: imagebroker.
net: pp. 12–13; Science and Society: p. 15, 21;
Bill Stevenson: p. 29; Tofoto: The Granger
Collection: pp. 30, 31, 36; © Look and Learn /
The Bridgeman Art Library: front cover

**Library and Archives Canada Cataloguing in Publication**

Hyde, Natalie,1963-, author
    Conquering Everest / Natalie Hyde.

(Crabtree chrome)
Includes index.
Issued in print and electronic formats.
ISBN 978-0-7787-1167-4 (bound).--ISBN 978-0-7787-1175-9
(pbk.).--ISBN 978-1-4271-8928-8 (pdf).--ISBN 978-1-4271-8920-2
(html)

    1. Hillary, Edmund, 1919-2008--Juvenile literature.
2. Tenzing Norkey, 1914-1986--Juvenile literature.
3. Mountaineering expeditions--Everest, Mount (China and
Nepal)--History--Juvenile literature. 4. Mountaineering--Everest,
Mount (China and Nepal)--Juvenile literature. 5. Mountaineers--
Juvenile literature. I. Title. II. Series: Crabtree chrome

GV199.44.E85H87 2013          j796.522095496     C2013-905241-0
                                                  C2013-905242-9

**Library of Congress Cataloging-in-Publication Data**

Hyde, Natalie, 1963-
  Conquering Everest / Natalie Hyde.
      pages cm. -- (Crabtree chrome)
  Includes index.
  ISBN 978-0-7787-1167-4 (reinforced library binding) --
ISBN 978-0-7787-1175-9 (pbk.) -- ISBN 978-1-4271-8928-8
(electronic pdf) -- ISBN 978-1-4271-8920-2 (electronic html)
1. Mountaineering expeditions--Everest, Mount (China
and Nepal)--History--Juvenile literature. 2. Mountaineers-
-Everest, Mount (China and Nepal)--Biography--Juvenile
literature. 3. Mallory, George, 1886-1924--Juvenile literature.
4. Hillary, Edmund, 1919-2008--Juvenile literature. 5.
Tenzing Norkey, 1914-1986--Juvenile literature. I. Title.

  GV199.44.E85H93 2014
  796.522095496--dc23

                                          2013030093

## Crabtree Publishing Company
www.crabtreebooks.com          1-800-387-7650

Printed in Canada/012014/BF20131120

Copyright © **2014 CRABTREE PUBLISHING COMPANY.** All rights reserved. No part of this publication may be
reproduced, stored in a retrieval system or be transmitted in any form or by any means, electronic, mechanical, photocopying,
recording, or otherwise, without the prior written permission of Crabtree Publishing Company. In Canada: We acknowledge
the financial support of the Government of Canada through the Canada Book Fund for our publishing activities.

**Published in Canada**
Crabtree Publishing
616 Welland Ave.
St. Catharines, ON
L2M 5V6

**Published in the United States**
Crabtree Publishing
PMB 59051
350 Fifth Avenue, 59th Floor
New York, New York 10118

**Published in the United Kingdom**
Crabtree Publishing
Maritime House
Basin Road North, Hove
BN41 1WR

**Published in Australia**
Crabtree Publishing
3 Charles Street
Coburg North
VIC 3058

# Contents

## A Historic Climb

Edmund Hillary and Tenzing Norgay stepped carefully along the frozen ridge. One wrong move and they would drop off the side of the mountain. Between them and the top of the mountain was a sheer wall of rock. Hillary wriggled up between the rock and ice.

## At the Top

Once above the rock step, they climbed a snowy dome and stood on top of Mount Everest. It was 11:30 a.m. on May 29, 1953. These two men had just made history. While Hillary took photographs, Norgay buried **offerings** of chocolate and biscuits to the mountain gods.

◀ *For more than 150 years, Mount Everest has attracted climbers who want to stand on the world's highest peak.*

"A few more whacks of the ice axe in the firm snow, and we stood on top."

Sir Edmund Hillary

**offerings:** gifts to the gods to give thanks or ask for something

# Earth's Highest Mountain

The **summit** of Mount Everest is higher than any other place on Earth. This huge mountain straddles the border between the countries of Nepal and Tibet in the mountain range known as the Himalayas. Everest draws people who like the thrill of adventure and who enjoy challenging themselves— sometimes even putting their lives at risk.

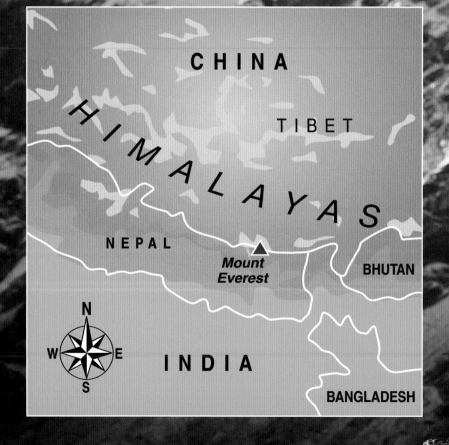

▲ *This map shows where Everest is in the Himalaya Mountains.*

## How the Himalayas Formed

Earth is made up of several giant plates, or landmasses, which move around very slowly. The Himalayas are fold mountains, which form when one plate pushes into another. This movement forces one landmass upward. The Himalayas were formed as India pushed north into Asia. They are the highest and youngest mountains in the world.

◀ *The Himalayan range is the highest in the world, with more than 100 mountains over 23,600 feet (7,200 meters) high.*

Earth's plates are always moving, and the Himalaya Mountains are still being pushed upward. Everest is growing at a rate of about one quarter inch (0.6 centimeters) each year.

**summit:** the very highest point

## Shaped by Nature

Mount Everest is shaped like a three-sided pyramid.
The steep sides have been carved out by wind, **avalanches**,
and glaciers. It stands 29,028 feet (8,848 meters) above sea
level. That is as high as 20 Empire State Buildings stacked
on top of each other, or 16 CN Towers!

▼ *There is a base camp on each
side of Everest—north and south.*

WAY TO MT. EVEREST B.C.

## Reaching Base Camp

Kathmandu is the capital of Nepal. Most brave climbers start their trek here. Hillary and his team walked for 17 days from Kathmandu to the starting point for their climb, known as base camp. Today, it takes about 10 hours to drive there, but most climbers fly from Kathmandu to the town of Lukla in Nepal, instead, which takes less time.

The Tenzing-Hillary Airport in Lukla is one of the most difficult airports in the world to fly in and out of. One end of the short runway ends at a mountain; the other ends in a 2,000-foot (600-meter) drop!

◀ *It takes a lot of skill for pilots to take off and land on the short runway in the mountain airport of Lukla.*

**avalanches:** large amounts of snow falling quickly down a mountain

# The Sherpa People

## Farmers and Traders

The Sherpas are the people native to the high mountain regions of Nepal. Before tourists came—attracted by the challenge of climbing Everest—the Sherpas were mainly farmers and traders. They were used to living in a high **altitude**. High in the mountains there is less oxygen than there is lower down, which makes it hard to breathe. It is also freezing cold. Sherpas are able to survive in these conditions.

▼ *Traditionally, the Sherpas were farmers, caring for herds of yak, or trading salt and wool.*

## Good Guides

The first foreign climbers who came to the Himalayas noticed that the Sherpas were incredibly strong. They could carry 50–80 pound (23–36 kilogram) packs up the mountains without difficulty. They were skilled at finding their way around the mountains. Climbers began hiring Sherpas to carry their equipment, fix ropes, and set up camps.

▶ *Sherpas are incredibly strong and can carry huge loads around the mountains.*

> "A Sherpa can carry a load for hours which a European can hardly lift."
>
> Writer Ian Cameron

**altitude:** something's height compared to sea level or ground level

# The Sacred Mountain

For the Sherpas, Mount Everest is a **sacred** place. They believe that in among the mountain peaks is *Shambhala*—a paradise where there are palaces and gardens. Before foreigners came, the Sherpas did not try and climb Everest themselves because it was the home of the gods.

▶ *This Sherpa is performing a ceremony to the goddess Miyo Langsangma, believed to live at the top of Mount Everest.*

▲ *Buddhist mantras (holy words) are painted or carved on rocks in the Himalayas.*

## Close to the Gods

Most Sherpa people follow a religion called Buddhism. They believe they should do things for others, not think only of themselves. That is why they often sacrifice their own safety. They do not climb the mountains for personal glory, but because they believe that the higher they are, the closer they are to the gods.

Before each climb, Sherpas perform the Puja ceremony. They ask permission from the gods to climb the mountain. They also ask for protection and blessings with offerings and prayers.

**sacred:** holy, connected with God

# "Because It's There"

## Looking Upward

Everest was identified as the highest mountain peak in the world in 1852. As soon as that fact became known, adventurous people wanted to climb it. They wanted to stand "on top of the world." It would be more than 100 years before someone finally achieved this great goal.

▶ *This view of the Himalaya Mountains from Mount Everest was drawn during the first survey of the region in the 1850s.*

# What's in a Name?

The first **surveyors** of the Himalayas, and Everest in particular, gave it the boring name "Peak 15." The British decided to rename it after Colonel George Everest. He was the head of the surveyors who were measuring the mountain range. Everest himself never liked the fact that it was named after him!

▶ *Sir George Everest carried out a huge survey of India and Nepal.*

The Sherpas in Tibet call the mountain *Chomolungma*, which means "Mother Goddess of the Land." In Nepal it is called *Sagarmatha*, which means "Head Touching the Sky."

**surveyors:** people who measure the area and altitude of land

## The First Attempt

In 1921, a British team became the first Europeans to set foot on Everest. But these men were not prepared for the harsh, freezing conditions on the mountain. They did not have the proper equipment and did not make it very far. However, their expedition did help map Everest for future climbers.

▼ *In 1924, another British team led by Edward Norton (front row second from left), tried to climb Everest. This time bad weather drove them off the mountain.*

## The North Face

All the early expeditions tried to reach the summit of Everest by climbing up the north ridge in Tibet. The south face of Everest is in Nepal. The Nepalese did not allow foreigners to **ascend** the mountain from this side.

▼ *The route up the north face includes the difficult Three Steps.*

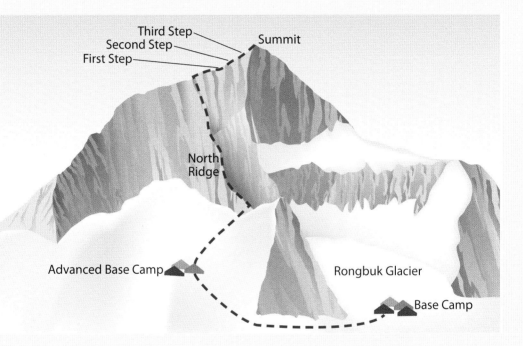

The north ridge includes the Three Steps. The First Step is made up of huge boulders. The Second Step is 130 feet (40 meters) high— some of it straight up. Climbers find the Third Step easier, as it's only 33 feet (10 meters) high!

**ascend:** climb

17

# Mallory and Irvine

Mountaineer George Mallory took part in both the early British attempts to climb Everest. He was determined to be the first climber to **conquer** the highest peak in the world. On June 8, 1924, he and his climbing partner Andrew Irvine set off up the north ridge. At noon they were spotted near the Second Step. That was the last anyone ever saw of them.

▶ *George Mallory (left) and Andrew Irvine (right). This is the last known photograph of the two men, as they set off on their fateful climb in 1924.*

Some people believe that Mallory and Irvine may have reached the summit before they died. Mallory carried a Kodak camera with him. Climbers still hope that one day this camera will be found, to prove whether Mallory and Irvine really were the first people to reach the summit.

## The Mystery (Partly) Solved

In 1999, a team was sent to look for their bodies. Mallory's body, preserved by the freezing temperatures, was finally found on May 1. Irvine's body was never found. A name tag on Mallory's jacket helped identify him. It was clear from his injuries he had died in a fall. What is not clear is whether it happened on the way up or on the way down.

**"Because it's there."**

George Mallory, on being asked why he wanted to climb Mount Everest

**conquer:** to beat something or overcome a challenge

## Altitude Sickness

At high altitudes there is less oxygen. This means that with each breath, the body takes in less oxygen than it does lower down. Without enough oxygen, people can get headaches, dizziness, and weakness, and they can have trouble breathing. At the highest altitudes, lack of oxygen can even cause the brain to swell.

▼ *These climbers are practicing using oxygen tanks before their attempt to climb Everest in 1953.*

# Gasping for Air

Altitude sickness was one of the biggest problems early climbers faced. They learned quickly that they needed special equipment if they were going to make it to the top. In 1922, they began taking oxygen in tanks along with them on climbs. These were heavy—but necessary if the climbers wanted to survive!

▼ *An oxygen tank from the 1920s next to a modern one. Sherpas called bottled oxygen "English Air." The first oxygen bottle sets weighed about 32 pounds (14.5 kilograms).*

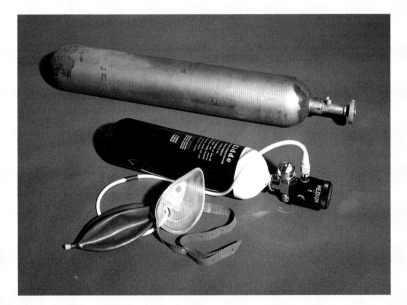

To **prevent** altitude sickness, climbers make practice treks between two of the lower camps several times before attempting to go higher. The only treatment for altitude sickness is to get to a lower altitude.

**prevent:** to stop something from happening

## Freezing Temperatures

Climbers also face problems with the cold temperatures. Frostbite happens when flesh freezes. Frostbitten flesh can turn gray and numb. Sometimes the flesh dies and rots away. Extreme cold can cause a dangerous drop in body temperature, resulting in **hypothermia**. In a very cold body, the organs shut down.

## Snow Blindness

Sunlight shining on white snow can be very bright. If climbers do not protect their eyes, they can suffer from snow blindness. With frostbite, hypothermia, or snow blindness, climbers can make mistakes. They can risk their lives by falling or going the wrong way.

◀ *The sunshine on the snow can affect climbers' eyesight.*

The summit of Everest lies in an area called the "Death Zone," which is any land above 26,000 feet (8,000 meters). At this altitude, the body cannot get used to the conditions. Climbers cannot stay in this zone for very long.

**hypothermia:** dangerously low body temperature

23

## Blown Away

The weather on Mount Everest can be harsh. Climbers can get lost in sudden snowstorms or thick fog. A band of extremely strong winds known as the jet stream can blow 177 miles per hour (285 kilometers per hour) across Everest. Mountaineers risk being blown right off a ridge in such strong winds.

▼ *Strong winds make it very dangerous for climbers on exposed parts of the mountain.*

# Cracks in the Ice

**Glaciers** change as they move and melt. The Khumbu Glacier on Everest advances about 3 feet (1 meter) each day. Crevasses are cracks in glaciers. They can be as thin as a rope or as wide as a highway. If a mountaineer falls down a crevasse, he or she can be killed or badly injured. Crevasses are often too deep to rescue fallen climbers.

Avalanches are sudden snow slides. They happen as frequently as every 48 hours on Everest. Half of all deaths on the mountain are caused by avalanches.

▲ *Some avalanches gather enough speed to tear down trees and move rocks as they crash down the mountain.*

**glaciers:** large, slow-moving rivers of ice

## Mapping the Mountain

Throughout the 1930s, several teams tried to make it up the north side of the mountain. All failed. The British explorer Eric Shipton led several important expeditions to Everest during this period. Although he never reached the summit, he took pictures of the mountain from many angles. This helped future climbers.

▶ *Eric Shipton and fellow explorers prepare to leave their snowy camp during an expedition in 1930.*

## Norgay's First Climb

On an expedition in 1935, Shipton hired the young Sherpa, Tenzing Norgay. Norgay soon proved his skills and usefulness. After that, he accompanied several British expeditions up Everest. One attempt in 1938 barely got going—**monsoon** weather came early, bringing massive amounts of snow.

> "Once you tried, it was very difficult to stop."
>
> Eric Shipton, talking about climbing Mount Everest

**monsoon:** a period of high winds and rainfall

# The World at War

World War II (1939–45) halted attempts to reach the summit of Mount Everest. After the war, China **invaded** Tibet and closed the country to tourists. But then Nepal opened up to foreigners. For the first time, climbers would make their way up the mountain from the south face.

▶ *A view of Everest from Nepal. It only became possible to access the mountain from the south side after the war.*

# The South Face

The south face of Everest has its own dangers. Climbers have to cross the Khumbu Icefall at the foot of the glacier. There, crevasses can form in a matter of minutes, swallowing up mountaineers. Ice blocks as big as houses can fall on climbers, crushing them.

▲ *Climbers use ladders to cross the deep crevasses in the dangerous Khumbu Icefall on the south face route.*

Many people have died on the slopes of Mount Everest. It is often impossible to retrieve the bodies and bring them down. Sherpas estimate that there are over 200 frozen bodies on the mountain from decades of tragic climbs.

**invaded:** took over by force

## The Swiss Attempt

The Nepalese government would allow only one expedition to try to summit the mountain each year. The British were eager to be the first in history to make it to the top. They were disappointed in 1952, when they learned that a Swiss team had been granted **permission** to make the climb. However, the Swiss failed to reach the peak.

▼ *After the failure of the Swiss expedition, another British team led by a former army officer, John Hunt, went back to the mountain.*

# Britain Gets a Chance

The British were determined not to lose out again. The next year, a team led by the British mountaineer John Hunt was told it had won the place. All together there were 13 members of the 1953 expedition, including a doctor and two experienced climbers—Edmund Hillary and Tenzing Norgay.

▼ *The successful 1953 team and their Sherpa guides.*

The best Sherpas were given an award called the "Tiger Medal" and earned the nickname Sherpa Tigers. Tenzing Norgay was one of the first Sherpas to win this award.

**permission:** the right to do something

# Tenzing Norgay

Tenzing Norgay was a Sherpa who had begun his career on the mountain as a **porter**, carrying heavy loads of equipment for different expeditions. Later he became a guide. Hunt decided to pair him with Hillary because they were both so experienced.

◀ *While preparing for the expedition, Norgay saved Hillary's life after he fell into a crevasse.*

"For in my heart I needed to go ... the pull of Everest was stronger for me than any force on Earth."

Tenzing Norgay

## Edmund Hillary

Edmund Hillary was born in New Zealand in 1919. He started climbing when was 20 years old, and was soon a skilled mountaineer. He went to Everest with a British surveying team sent to map the mountain in 1951. Hillary's experience and knowledge of Everest made him a natural choice for Hunt's team in 1953.

▲ *After Everest, Edmund Hillary reached both the North and South Poles, becoming the first person to reach all three.*

**porter:** a person hired to carry loads

## At Base Camp

It took the team two months just to get from England to base camp at the foot of Everest. Over 350 porters—both men and women—carried the equipment from Kathmandu to Everest. To set up camp, the team needed tents, food, fuel, clothing, and climbing gear. Each pack weighed about 50 pounds (23 kilograms).

▶ *Porters carried the team's equipment across the dangerous Khumbu Glacier on the way to base camp.*

"We agreed that this was going to be no ordinary climb. For the time being, Everest was rather more than a mountain."

Expedition leader John Hunt

## First Failure

On May 7, 1953, after weeks of preparation, Hunt finally named the two pairs of explorers who would make the summit attempt. The first team to try was Charles Evans and Tom Bourdillon. They ran out of oxygen before they reached the top. Exhausted and **dejected**, the two men came back down the mountain, where their friends were eagerly waiting for news.

**dejected:** very unhappy

# Preparing for the Summit

All hopes of success now lay with Hillary and Norgay. On May 28, 1953, two days after the first failure, team members helped them set up a camp high on the south **col**. From here they would begin the last part of the climb. Neither of them slept well that night. It was freezing cold, and both men were anxious about what lay ahead.

▼ *It took a huge effort for the two men to climb the last few feet to the summit, but they knew they had to do it.*

Hillary: "What do you think of it, Tenzing?" Norgay: "Very bad. Very dangerous."

Hillary and Norgay, as they climbed to the summit.

## Everest Conquered

In the morning, Hillary had to thaw his boots over the stove. Norgay melted snow for water. At 6:30 a.m. they set off for the summit. Finding it hard to breathe, they struggled through the ice and snow with their oxygen tanks. At 11:30 a.m., exhausted but still determined, they realized that there were no more ridges to climb. They had made it to the "top of the world."

▼ *Hillary and Norgay, after they finally reached the summit of Mount Everest.*

**col:** a ridge between two peaks

# Everest Today

## A Popular Challenge

Today, the Nepalese government allows more than one expedition a year, and many people cannot resist the challenge of the world's highest mountain. Since Hillary and Norgay's historic climb, well over 5,000 people have stood at the summit of Everest.

▲ *Sometimes the route up Everest is so crowded that not everyone can fit on the highest point!*

## First Female

The first woman to reach Everest's summit was Junko Tabei of Japan. During her climb in 1975, Tabei's tent was buried under an avalanche high on the slopes. A Sherpa dug her out, and she continued her journey to the top. The person who has summited more than anyone else is a mountaineer from Nepal named Apa Sherpa. Nicknamed Super Sherpa, he has stood at the peak 21 times so far!

The oldest, youngest, and fastest records for climbing Everest change nearly every year. Climbers are finding new ways up and down the mountain, including on **paragliders** and skis.

**paragliders:** large sails with a harness hanging below for the rider

# Modern Equipment

Today's climbers have things a bit easier than Hillary and Norgay did in 1953. Climbing equipment has changed a lot since then. Clothing is warmer and more **flexible**. Ropes, ladders, and picks are lighter and stronger. Oxygen tanks are also much lighter. This makes the final distance to the summit much easier and safer to climb.

▼ *Today, mountaineers have specially made clothes and a lot of modern equipment to help them.*

It costs about $50,000 to climb Everest. Some of the money goes to improve the lives of local people. Schools, roads, and hospitals are built with the funds.

## Rules of the Mountain

More and more people are attempting to summit Everest each year. This has started to spoil the beauty of the mountain. Litter at base camp and on the trails has become a huge problem. New rules force expeditions to bring back all their garbage or face stiff fines.

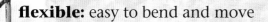

**flexible:** easy to bend and move

# Deaths on the Mountain

Reaching the summit of Mount Everest is a huge accomplishment. It comes with huge risks, though. Many people have died trying. The deadliest year on record was 1996. The crowded slopes meant many climbers had to spend too much time in the "Death Zone." Ninety-eight people reached the top that year, but 15 died.

▼ *Memorials for people who have died on the mountain have been been built of stone along the route.*

IN MEMORY OF
PETER LEGATE
8 OCT 1963 30
APR 2009 MOUNT
EVEREST

# Exposure

Reaching the summit of Everest is only half the battle. Many deaths happen on the way back down. Robert Hall was an experienced climber and guide. In 1996, he phoned his wife from the summit to tell her he had made it to the top safely. Sadly, he died of **exposure** on the mountainside on the return journey.

▼ *Sherpas carry an injured climber down the mountain.*

Mountaineer Bruce Herrod's body was found hanging by a place called Hillary Step. It had to be cut down so others could get past. The next year, Herrod's camera was found with pictures of him on the summit.

**exposure:** being unprotected from heat or cold

## A Rocky Summit

Climbing Everest is more popular now than it has ever been, but the Sherpas are seeing changes on the mountain. Our world is getting warmer. This means that on Everest and other mountains, there is less snow and more exposed rock on the peak. It is more dangerous for climbers, because of the risks of **rock falls**. Rock is also more slippery than snow.

▶ *As it gets warmer in the mountains, more and more slippery rocks are exposed.*

In 2003, on the 50th anniversary of Hillary and Norgay's amazing climb, a special team reached the summit of Everest. Hillary's son, Peter, and Tenzing Norgay's son, Jamling, stood together on the peak, honoring their fathers.

## Medical Research

Researchers are heading to Mount Everest to do studies. The human body struggles with muscle loss and breathing in the "Death Zone." These problems are similar to what happens when a person has heart disease. Doctors hope that by studying the conditions on the mountain they can learn how the body might recover from such diseases.

**rock falls:** rocks and stones falling down a cliff

# Learning More

## Books

*Hillary and Norgay: To the Top of Mount Everest*
by Heather Whipple
(Crabtree, 2007)

*Mount Everest*
by Valerie Bodden
(Franklin Watts, 2011)

*The Top of the World: Climbing Mount Everest*
by Steve Jenkins
(Sandpiper, 2002)

*Tales from the Top of the World: Climbing Mount Everest with Pete Athans*
by Sandra K. Athans
(Lerner Publishing, 2012)

*You Wouldn't Want to Climb Mount Everest!: A Deadly Journey to the Top of the World*
by Ian Graham
(Franklin Watts, 2010)

*Mount Everest*
by Sarah De Capua
(Children's Press, 2002)

## Websites

*www.youtube.com/watch?v=r9MzCup-jnA*
Video of Sir Edmund Hillary and Tenzing Norgay's conquest of Everest

*www.alanarnette.com/kids/everestfacts.php*
Everest Facts for Kids

*http://kids.nationalgeographic.com/kids/games/geographygames/quizyournoodle-mount-everest/*
Quiz Your Noodle: Mount Everest

*www.thefreeresource.com/cool-facts-about-mount-everest-for-kids*
Cool Facts about Mount Everest

# Glossary

**altitude** Something's height compared to sea level or ground level

**ascend** Climb

**avalanches** Large amounts of snow falling quickly down a mountain

**col** A ridge between two peaks

**conquer** To beat something or overcome a challenge

**dejected** Very unhappy

**exposure** Being unprotected from heat or cold

**flexible** Easy to bend and move

**glaciers** Large, slow-moving rivers of ice

**hypothermia** Dangerously low body temperature

**invaded** Took over by force

**monsoon** A period of high winds and rainfall

**offerings** Gifts to the gods to give thanks or ask for something

**paragliders** Large sails with a harness hanging below for the rider

**permission** The right to do something

**porter** A person hired to carry loads

**prevent** To stop something from happening

**rock falls** Rocks and stones falling down a cliff

**sacred** Holy, connected with God

**summit** The very highest point

**surveyors** People who measure the area and altitude of land

# Index

Entries in **bold** refer to pictures